Published by:
Arabesque Int.

Text:
Meg Abu-Hamdan

Editor:
Julie-Ann Tertinegg

Designer:
Khader Naim

Photos:
Ali Kettaneh
Adam Comb
Youssef Allan
Haitham Jwainat

First Edition: June 1993

CONTENTS   PAGE

THE HISTORY

To walk in Jordan is to tread on history. There is archaeological evidence of settlements dating back to the Paleolithic Age, and on-going excavations are constantly bringing to light signs of habitation across time through the present

The Kingdom has been a major site for civilization throughout recorded history. In 331 BC, Alexander the Great's armies conquered the Near East and introduced Hellenistic culture to the area. On the death of Alexander in 323 BC, the Greek Empire was divided between his two generals, Ptolemy and Seleucus. Jordan, Palestine, and Egypt were given to Ptolemy.

Between 400 BC and 160 AD, the independent southern kingdom of the Nabataeans flourished. Their awesome capital of Perta is Jordan's most popular tourist attraction.

Between 63 and 324 AD, Jordan belonged to the Roman Empire. The Graeco-Roman cities of Jerash, Philadelphia

Statue of Ammonite King (Iron Age)

Ammonite female heads (7th century BC)

Painted Nabataean pottery (First century AD)

Amman, Um Qais, and Pella were four cities of the commercially significant Decapolis, a league of ten cities established to facilitate the trade and commerce of the area.

During the Byzantine period, 324-632 AD, the inhabitants of Jordan cultivated their land and sold provisions to travellers on the caravan routes linking China, India and Southern Arabia, with Syria, Egypt and the Mediterranean.

The Arab-Islamic period started in 630. The Umayyad and Abbasid dynasties of Damascus and Baghdad ruled the area for 250 years. In 1099, the Crusaders established themselves in Jerusalem and built two large castles in Jordan, at Kerak and Shobak, to protect their conquests. In 1178, Salah Al Din (Saladin) defeated the Crusaders at Kerak, a preclude to their complete withdrawal from the Near East. Following a 300-year rule by the Mamelukes, Jordan became part of the Ottoman Empire, under which it remained until the time of the famous Arab Revolt, beginning in 1915 and ending in 1918.

The modern history of Jordan can be dated from 1921 when Emir Abdullah, second son of Sherif Hussein of the Hejaz, established the

Um Qais - portrait

Emirate of Trans-Jordan. It was a self-governing territory under the Bristish Mandate. In 1928, the Anglo-Trans-Jordanian treaty was signed providing for the establishment of a legislative assembly with limited powers.

On May 25, 1946, Emir Abdullah was proclaimed King of the newly independent Hashemite Kingdom of Jordan. In 1950, the formal union of Jordan and the West Bank was declared.

On August 11, 1925, King Abdullah's 17 - year - old grandson, Hussein Ibn Talal, became King. The young Monarch formally acceded the throne in 1953.

Umm er-Rassas -

Nabataean pottery - Petra

218   216

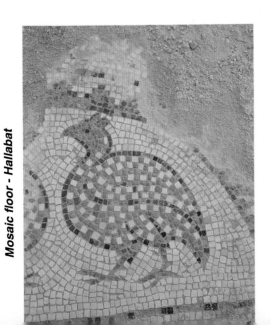

Mosaic floor - Hallabat

THE PEOPLE

Throughout Jordan's history, the Bedouins of the Jordanian desert have upheld their traditional way of life. Their livelihood, unchanged for the past millenia, is shepherding their huge flocks of sheep and goats, which they seasonally move to fresh pastures. The men spend their days tending the flocks, leading them with the aid of a donkey and dogs from one ancient stone well to another. In the evening they return to their black, goat hair tents which can be seen dotted throughout the countryside. The simple furnishings of their homes, the cushion and mattress covers, the rugs and storage bags are hand-woven by the women on ground looms set up outside the tents in the spring. A fire burns constantly, over which the men prepare coffee. Passers-by are always hailed and invited to share a cup of the strong, bitter liquid or even to partake in their traditional meal of mansaf - - lamb cooked in yoghurt and served on a bed of rice. The legendary Arab hospitality is no myth and has to be experienced to be fully appreciated.

Although village life has in recent years

Desert Police Patrol

changed more radically than that of the nomad, it remains in essence the same. The older women of the village, and sometimes the younger ones too, still make and wear the traditonal dress - - a long black thobe, with hems, yokes and sleeves decorated with tiny embroidered stitches that form intricate and colourful patterns. Out in the fields age-old methods of farming are still employed. Although these are being gradually replaced by more modern techniques it is not uncommon to see men winnowing the grain with rough wooden implements or a group of women on their haunches methodically cutting the corn with small, hand scyths. The springtime sight of a farmer behind his horse and plough gives the Jordanian countryside a sense of timelessness and the feeling of restful continuity.

Even in the cities, traditional values have not lost their ways. From an early age Jordanians are taught to be generous, warm, open and friendly, and at the core of the Jordanian society remain the ideals of tribal unity and respect for the family.

Road To Um Qais & Hammeh

Wadi Rum

THE COUNTRY

Jordan offers a tremendous variety of things to see and do. Among the rolling forrested hills of the north are many fascinating, ancient sites. There are the beautiful and monumental ruins of Roman Jerash; the Arab castle of Qal'at al Rabad, perched on a hilltop overlooking the village of Ajloun; Madaba, with its Byzantine churches and mosaics; Salt, which boasts its old Ottoman houses rising up the hillside; and Mount Nebo and Um Qais, each with its own unsurpassed view over the surrounding countryside.

Further out in the eastern desert there are the lonely and mysterious desert castles as well as the wetlands of Azraq where millions of migratory birds rest annually. It is in Azraq's wildlife reserve that the fabled Arabian oryx and ostrich wander.

Moving west, is the Jordan Valley with its many rich archaeological sites among which is Pella, whose extensive ruins spread over picturesque hills and valleys. The Dead Sea, nearby, at 400 metres below sea level, is the lowest point on Earth.

A journey south will take one past the great

Azraq Oasis

Arabian oryx, Azraq

Houses in Salt

Crusader castles of Kerak and Shobak and then onto one of the most famous ancient cities in the world - - Petra. No amount of photographs or information can prepare one for the vastness, beauty and mystery of this wonder. Hidden behind a barrier of stunningly beautiful mountains, Petra, the city of the Nabataeans, is approached down a long and narrow gorge whose vertical sides all but obliterate the sun. The gorge opens out into a dazzlingly bright natural square, dominated by the vast pink facade of the Khasneh (the Treasury). Past the Khasneh, the ancient city spreads out for kilometre after kilometer in a never-ending series of intricately carved facades. Rock-cut stairs, hidden behind brightly flowering oleander, lead one on to further monuments.

Beyond Petra is the stark beauty of Wadi Rum, where one can climb the huge mountain masses that rise vertically out of the sand, and later camp under the stars.

At the very southern end of the country is the holiday resort of Aqaba. Here in the crystal clear waters of the Red Sea are found some of the most spectacular coral reefs in the world. The water-front hotels offer facilities for

Asphodel flowers at Petra

Wadi Rum

Folklore performances at the Jerash Festival

all kinds of water sports, from wind surfing to water skiing, while the two main diving centres provide equipment and courses for snorkelling and scuba diving.

The perfect base from which to make trips to explore the rich history and monuments of Jordan is Amman, the thriving modern capital.

Amman's plentiful five-star and four-star hotels, its international airport, its modern telecommunications system, its many Arab, continental and oriental restaurants, and - above all - its thousand-year-old traditiom of hospitality make it an efficient, comfortable jumping - off point for visiting the magnificent sites of Jordan.

Aerial view of Amman

Kerak Castle

CITIES OF THE SOUTH

MADABA

Just 20 minutes south of Amman, on the Kings' Highway, is the mosaic-filled city of Madaba. Crowned by a small church, this historic town lies in the middle of Jordan's most fertile land.

In many respects Madaba is a typical East Bank town which differs in one major aspect: underneath almost every house lies a fine Byzantine mosaic. Many of these mosaics have been excavated and are on display in the town's museum, but it is estimated that many more lie hidden waiting to be discoverd.

A cosmetic container (5th century AD)

The finest mosaic found to date is still in its original place on the floor of the Greek Orthodox Church of St. George. This huge well - preserved work of art comprises a map of the entire region from Jordan and Palestine in

The Apostles' church - Madaba (578 AD)

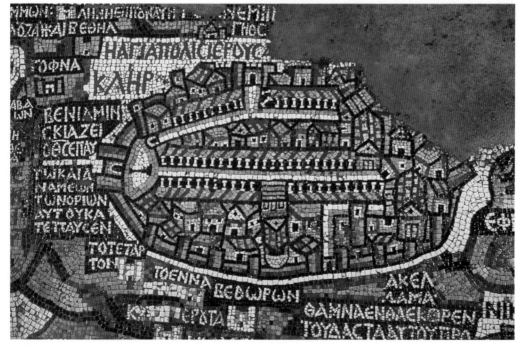

Mosaics at khirbet al Mukhayat

the north, to Egypt in the south. Many towns and cities are depicted in picture form, complete with walls and pitched red-roofed houses, while in the Nile huge fish swim.

Madaba is also famous for its handwoven rugs which are made in small street-front workshops on upright looms in modern and traditional colours and designs.

MOUNT NEBO

Situated 10 kilometres west of Madaba, overlooking the Jordan Valley is Mount Nebo, one of the alleged sites of the tomb of Moses. The summit of this lonely windswept site command spectacular views over the Dead Sea to the West Bank and Jerusalem and, you can see the springs where Moses smote the ground to bring forth water.

Standing amongst extensive ruins is a small church which protects some fine and beautifully preserved sixth century mosaics which are still being uncovered.

Zerqa Ma'in thermal spring

ZERQA MA'IN

A short drive south of Madaba is the newly built Ma'in Spa, constructed on the site of the hot mineral springs where Herod the Great and subsequent rulers took their cures. The hotel there offers thermal pools and trained physiotherapists to provide professional services and guidance to those seeking the curative powers of the waters.

MUKAWIR

Just 15 kilometres south of Madaba, crowning the summit of a barren isolated site, are the impressive remains of a Roman fortress built by Herod the Great. It was here that John the Baptist was imprisoned and where he was finally beheaded to fulfill the wish of the beautiful Salome.

KERAK

Dominating the walled city of Kerak is a massive Crusader castle built on a craggy plateau 4,300 feet above sea level. Constructed in 1136

Citadel of Machaerus

as part of a long line of Crusader mountain-top castles that defended the route from Aqaba in the south to Turkey in the north, *Crac de moab* is a staggering feat of human achievement. Constructed in huge blocks of stone on top of a precipice, the castle stands four stories high. Inside the fortification is a labyrinth of cross-vaulted galleries, stables, halls, towers and secret passages. The Crusaders managed to hold it for 50 years until 1189, when Salah Al Din (Saladin) defeated the foreigners.

SHOBAK

Situated some 20 kilometres north of Petra is the Crusader castle of Shobak. Built around 1115, it was besieged repeatedly by Saladin and finally captured in 1189. Perched on a mountain top, the castle is reached by a narrow road which affords spectacular views of the surrounding barren hillsides. Except for its outside walls, square keep, and a dungeon, the castle is virtually a ruin.

The Crusadar castle at Shobak

Kerak Castle-an interior view

PETRA

Hidden behind an almost impenetrable barrier of rugged mountains, the rock-carved city of Petra is full of mysterious charm. The approach through the cool gloom of the Siq, a long narrow gorge whose steeply rising sides all but obliterate the sun, provides a dramatic contrast with the magic to come. Suddenly the gorge opens into a natural square dominated by Petra's most famous monument, the Khasneh, whose intricately carved facade glows in the dazzling sun. More facades beckon the visitor on until the ancient city gradually unfolds, one monument leading on to the next for kilometre after kilometre. The sheer size of the city and the quality of beautifully carved facades is staggering and leads one to reflect on the creativity and industry of the Nabataeans who made Petra their capital more than 2,000 years ago.

The Nabataeans were an Arabic-speaking people who moved into south Jordan in the late 7th century, early 6th century BC. Because of its strategic location across the "Silk and Spice Routes", Petra was established as their capital in the 2nd century AD. At the height of its power,

Wild flowers of Petra

the city had a population of more than 25,000 people. Petra prospered for many centuries but after control of the trade routes was taken over by the 7th century BC, the ancient city was the home of only a few shepherds and so it remained for several centuries; the fabled city existing only as a legend until it was rediscovered by the Anglo-Swiss explorer, John Lewis Burckhardt in 1812.

Dionysos basrelief - Petra.

Bedul Bedouins at Petra

Beida: Neolithic village

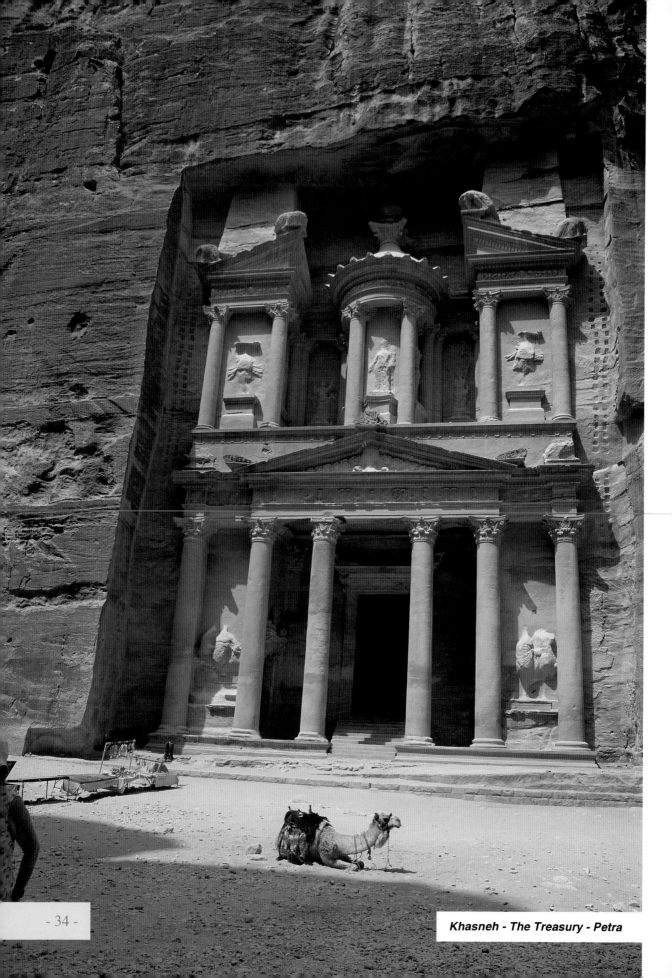

Khasneh - The Treasury - Petra

Khasneh

Rock formation - Petra

Colonnaded Street - Petra

Theatre - Petra

The High Place of Sacrifice

Al - Deir - Nabataean Monument

AQABA

The small Red Sea port of Aqaba is unique and beautiful in a very special way. Encircled by rugged purple mountains that subtly change in mood and colour as the day unfolds, the still, calm waters of the bay glisten under a beaming sun. Early in the morning, all is quiet, the only sound is the gentle lapping of waves breaking on the sandy beach. Then slowly, as the town awakens, the sea becomes alive with a flotilla of craft dodging around the great cargo ships patiently awaiting their turn to enter the port. Motor boats roar by, pulling waterskiers in their wake, and sailing silently out to sea is a lone

Water skiing & diving - Aqaba

Ski festival - Aqaba

wind surfer. On the beaches visitors soak up the sun before cooling off in the refreshingly cool waters.

It is the secrets these waters hold that make Aqaba unique, for further down the coast are some of the most spectacular coral reefs to be found anywhere in the world. Often over many hundreds of metres wide, the reef is made up of many delicately hued corals among which live a myriad of brilliantly coloured fish. Shimmering shoals of Damsel fish turning in unison swim by Parrot fish lingering in crevices, while the deeper waters are home to huge manta rays, turtles and sharks. The crystal clear waters of the Red Sea mean that visibility below the water is excellent and the reefs are a paradise for both snorkelers and scuba divers. Full facilities and courses of instruction are provided by two diving centres.

The town of Aqaba is ancient in origin; the first settlement in the area dating back more than 6,000 years. The Fortress, now a museum, was originally a Crusader Castle. It was extensively rebuilt by the Mamelukes in the 14th century.

A stroll around the modern town will reveal the presence of some excellent fish restaurants and craftsmen are to be found at work filling small bottles with coloured sand in intricate geometric designs.

Underwater - Red Sea - Aqaba

WADI RUM

Some 70 kilometres northeast of Aqaba lies Wadi Rum, a vast silent place that is both romantic and starkly beautiful. Massive mountains rise vertically out of the pink desert sand, which separates one dark mass from another. The faces of these sheer rock cliffs have been eroded by the wind into faces of men, animals and monsters.

Everywhere in this strange and empty place are indications of man's presence since the earliest known times. Scattered around are flint hand-axes, while on the rocks at the feet of the mountains the names of ancient travellers are scratched. In the centre of the valley an elaborately carved temple bears witness that Wadi Rum was once a holy place for the Nabataeans. The entrance to the valley is guarded by the famous Desert Patrol.

Sunset, Haroun

Theatre - Petra

The High Place of Sacrifice

drawing and inscriptions

AMMAN

AN ANCIENT MODERN CITY

Amman is a fast-growing, expanding capital city of a young Arab kingdom - the Hashemite Kingdom of Jordan. Founded as the capital in 1912, Amman is now a thriving modern city.

Down in the city centre are the traditional Arab souks - - narrow streets lined with tiny shops selling everything from heavy gold bracelets to headdresses. In between are the coffee shops, kiosks selling freshly squeezed juices, and restaurants where one can buy felafel sandwiches and delicious Arabic sweets. Also downtown is the magnificent Roman amphitheatre whose vaults house two of Amman's museums: the Popular Museum of Costume and Jewellery and the Folklore Museum.

Overlooking the amphitheatre on top of Citadel Hill are more reminders of Amman's long and varied history. Around the Archaeological Museum are the ruins of the great Roman Temple of Her-

The Martyrs' Monument

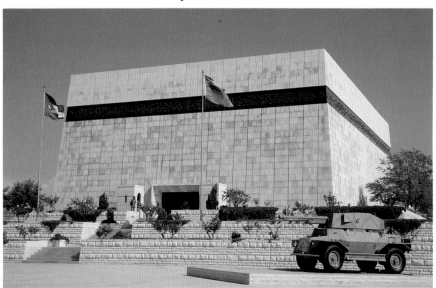

The Roman Temple of Hercules, Amman

cules, and of an early Islamic Palace. Away from downtown, the character of the city changes. In the modern suburbs are limestone villas, air conditioned office blocks and first class hotels. In Amman all the facilities and conveniences of the twentieth century are greatly enhanced by the traditional sense of Arab hospitality.

The most impressive of Amman's many mosques is the King Abdullah Mosque. Inaugurated in 1989, the mosque is a masterpiece of modern Islamic design. Housed beneath the massive blue dome is the great prayer hall whose walls are clad with hand-carved mashrabieh and panels of inlaid marble. During the day, the hall is softly lit by the sunlight filtering through the stained glass windows that line the drum of the dome. At night, prayer is performed under the glow of a great chandelier. The complex with its towering twin minarets also includes a conference hall, a royal pavilion and a Koranic school.

Several times a year on special occasions, the bands of the Jordan Armed Forces "Beats the Retreat". Spectacular in their colourful uniforms, the bands march as they play. The lively

Al - Fath Mosque, Amman

King Abdullah Mosque, Amman

Arab Horses.

and energetic music is enhanced by several musicans playing the bagpipes.

In the rolling wooded countryside just outside the capital is the Royal State Stud where some of the most beautiful Arabian horses in the world are stabled. Founded by His Majesty King Hussein in 1961, the stud is now run by his daughter Princess Alia whose main concern is to maintain the purity of the Arabian horse in its original environment.

Kan Zaman - Once Upon a Time - is the name given to a new complex of craft shops and restaurants all housed in lovely hundred - year - old farm buildings and located 15 kilometres from Amman on the airport highway not far from the Royal State Stud. Delicious Arabic cuisine is served in the renovated barrel - vaulted stables, while in other restored outhouses are shops selling spices, bread, ceramic ware and glass which is hand-blown as you watch.

THE MUSEUMS OF AMMAN

The rich heritage of Jordan's past civilizations and the variety of its contemporary culture can both be appreciated by visiting the museums and craft centres of Amman. The most important

Hand - woven rugs - the Bani Hamida Project.

Sand bottler at work   **Restaurant Kan Zaman - Amman**

ones include:

o ***The Amman Archaeological Museum -*** a small, but well-arranged and rich collection of artifacts from the past 500,000 years of human history. Located on Citadel Hill, adjacent to the Roman and Islamic monuments, the museums' collection is arranged in chronological order. You can easily appreciate the collection in a visit of one or two hours. Open daily except Tuesday.

o ***Jordan Museum of Popular Traditions -*** located in the east vaults of the Roman theatre, includes a full exhibition of traditional Jordanian costumes, jewellery, rugs and everyday utensils and implements. Open daily.

o ***Amman Folklore Museum -*** located in the west vaults of the theatre, takes you into the colourful world of the desert-dwelling Bedouins and the villagers of Jordan. Open daily except Tuesday.

o ***The Jordan Craft Centre,*** located on a small side street off the Second Circle of Jabal Amman, behind the Lebanese embassy, exhibits and sells the most complete collection of traditional and authentic, Jordanian crafts, including embroidery, woodwork, glass, leather, woven

Amman Citadel Umayyad palace

Umayyad bazero from Al Fedeir (Mafraq)

*Tell Siran inscribed bronze bottle
(Amman 6th Century BC)*

rugs, sheepskins, ceramics, mother-of-pearl objects, stonework, jewellery, brass and silver. Open daily except Fridays.

o *Jordan National Gallery* - located in Jebal Luweibdeh next to the public gardens, includes a permanent collection of contemporary art and ceramics from Jordan and the Arab and Islamic world. Open daily.

o *The Martyrs' Monument and Military Museum* - housed in a distinctive square building on a hill overlooking the Hussein Sports City, includes a fine permanent exhibition of Jordan's military history. Open daily except Saturday.

'IRAQ Al EMIR

Twenty-four kilometres west of Amman, in a lush valley kept green by the cool waters of its perennial spring, lie the ruins of one of the most important Hellenistic monuments in the Middle East: 'Iraq al Emir, meaning "the caves of the prince". The focal point of the site is the reconstructed palace of a local Arab-Hellenistic ruler named Hyrcanus, built in the early 2nd century BC. The two-storey-high building was once

'Iraq Al Emir, Wadi el Seer

richly adorned with carved lions and panthers (several of which remain intact) and its second story was ringed by fluted Corinthian columns and a frieze of lions and lionesses. The whole structure was surrounded by a defensive moat. The building is called Qasr al Abd, or "castle of the slave", referring to its owner as the servant, or slave, of the king.

Archaeological excavations prove the site was inhabited as far back as the Chalcolithic period, about 6,000 years ago, and defensive walls dating from the Iron Age (around 1050 BC) have also been identified. Pottery and a sculptured lion's head show the site was inhabited during the Persian era (4th to 6th centuries BC), When the Tobiah family ruled the region of modern Jordan. Another Tobiah ruled in the region in the mid-3rd century BC. In the hillside north of the palace, a series of eleven man-made caves seems to have been used for both human and animal shelter. The name Tobiah, in an ancient Aramaic script of the 3rd century BC is inscribed at the entrance of two of the caves.

The modern village at 'Iraq al Emir, 600 metres northeast of the castle, is also dotted with the remains of ancient installations, including a water cistern, a wine press system and several thick defensive walls.

You can drive to 'Iraq al Emir by car in about 30 minutes, taking the road west of Amman that passes through the village of Wadi el Seer. There are no formal services at the site, but its proximity to Amman and the lushness of its setting in a green, water-filled valley make it a favourite spot for picnickers.

Turkish houses

Aerial view of the south theatre, Jerash

CITIES OF THE DECAPOLIS

JERASH

A visit to the spectacular Roman ruins of Jerash immediately transports the visitor two thousand years back in time. The city's many splendid monumental remains still retain the atmosphere of the once thriving metropolis, famous in its own time for magnificent temples, theatres, and plazas.

From these buildings and the many other well-preserved structures, it is easy to imagine the city in its heyday: Down the colonnaded streets, chariots would have trundled, their wheels etching ever deeper the already weel-worn grooves. The little shops that line the street would have stocked exotic goods brought in from Persia, Egypt and the bustle of the city would have been punctuated by other sounds; the gentle splash of water flowing from the fountains of the Nymphaeum; the tapping of builders and masons at work; and the occasional roar of a satisfied crowd

Carved sarcophagus - Jerash

The Birkitein pools, Jerash

being entertained in the amphitheatres. Although now in ruins the spirit of Roman Gerasa lives on.

The Nymphaeum, Jerash

UM QAIS

On a plateau overlooking the north Jordan Valley and the glinting blue waters of Lake Tiberias are the ruins of Qais, ancient Roman Gadara. Although not as extensive as the other cities of the Roman League of the Decapolis (the "Ten Cities"), already uncovered are the ruins of three theatres, a temple, a colonnaded street and an aqueduct. Archaeologists predict that when excavations are complete, a major city will have been uncovered. Standing atop the largest of the theatres, one has an excellent view of Lake Tiberias (Sea of Galilee), northern Palestine and the Golan Heights.

It was in Gadara that Jesus vanquished demonic spirits into the sea far below. Gadara was also the home and birthplace of many Roman writers and philosophers who were inspired by the beauty of the panaromic views that spread out all around them. They enjoyed, as people do today, the hot water springs that bubble up in the nearby village of Hammeh.

Terrace of the Basilical

Roman Byzantine - Um Qais
Marble statue of Tyche

Restored Turkish house
(Beit al Rousan)

AJLOUN

Overlooking the village of Ajloun, situated some 24 kilometres northwest of Jerash is the beautifully preserved Arab castle, Qala'at al-Rabad.

One of the best examples of Arab military architecture to be found in Jordan, this ancient fortress was built in 1184 AD by one of the Ayyubite Sultan Saladin's generals, Isseddin Usama, as defence against the Crusaders. Perched dramatically on the highest hilltop in the area, the castle commands spectacular views across the Jordan Valley and the Biblical land of Gilead.

Ajloun Castle

UM EL JIMAL

The Roman-Byzantine-Umayyad city of Um el Jimal ("mother of the camel") was built on an earlier Nabataean settlement and is constructed of square cut basalt rocks, supported by solid, rectangular basalt beams. Because of the few standing walls and the masses of piled rocks, from a distance it looks much like a bombed-out city.

Um el Jimal is believed to have been a caravan staging post. Located just east of Mafraq, near the Syrian border, it lay in close proximity to a number of ancient cities and therefore could well have served this purpose.

One interesting feature is the numerous cisterns, household ones. It is still a mystery as to precisely how the people of Um el Jimal acquired their water, as it is far from any evident sources. But there are ground level aqueducts, so it is thought they enterprisingly hauled it over many miles.

Um el Jimal

The River Jordan

THE DEAD SEA

&

THE JORDAN VALLEY

Running down the full length of Jordan, forming a natural western boundary, is the Jordan Rift Valley. It is accessible through Irbid, Ajloun, Salt and Naur in the northern and central area, and through Kerak and Aqaba from the south. The descent into the valley along any route affords panoramic scenes only to be imagined, and if in the springtime, the blossoms alone make the drive worthwhile.

With its plentiful natural resources, this valley has been the site of human occupation from the earliest known times. The most spectacular site however, is the Dead Sea, which at 400 metres below sea level is the lowest body of water on earth.

Surrounded by arid hills, as devoid of life as the sea itself, the Dead Sea glistens under a boiling sun with barely a ripple disturbing its surface. The rocks that meet its lapping edges become covered with a snow-like thick gleaming deposit of white salt. It is this extremely high concentration of salt that gives the Dead Sea waters their renowned thera-

The River Mujib

**The Roman Odeon of Pella
(Foreground)**

peutic qualities and their buoyancy. Swimming in the Dead Sea is a truly unique experience not to be missed.

PELLA

In the warm, well-watered, richly fertile lands of the north Jordan Valley lie the remains of ancient Pella - one of Jordan's largest archaeological sites. Pella has been continuously inhabited for more than six thousand years, and visible ruins date from Hellenistic, Roman and Byzantium times, when the city was a flourishing commercial centre with links to all the main trading cities in the eastern Mediterranean area. Earlier remains include several Bronze Age tombs. Hewn out of the rock these tombs once contained many hundreds of everyday and luxury objects - - to help the dead on their journey into the afterlife. Set in some of Jordan's prettiest countryside, Pella is at its most lovely in the spring when the valley floors are carpeted with wild flowers.

Umayyad quarter, Pella

Pella, Tabaqat Fahl

HISTORIC PALACES

&

CASTLES

Lying in the desert east of Amman are a number of desert castles built or restored in the seventh and eighth centuries by the Umayyad caliphs. Constructed as both retreats of pleasure and bastions of protection, they stand as a memorial to the early days of the Arab Empire.

QASR HALLABAT

A magnificent ruin, Qasr Hallabat was originally an early 2nd Century AD Roman fort or watchtower that helped protect the western hills and plains of Jordan against marauding attackers from the east. Inscriptions in the castle show it was rebuilt as a major installation during the reign of the Roman Emperor Caracalla, around 212-215 AD. It was refurbished once again in the Byzantine period, and finally reached its height as an Umayyad complex during the 7th and 8th cnturies AD. The Umayyad patrons of the castle

Entrance to Qasr Hallabat

8th century mosque at Qasr Hallabat

decorated it in elaborate mosaics, carved stucco, wood and frescoes.

The Hallabat complex faded soon after the Umayyad dynasty came to an end in the middle of the 8th Century AD, when the Abbasid dynasty ruled the Islamic Empire from the new capital in Baghdad.

QASR AZRAQ

An hour's drive east of Amman is the desert oasis of Azraq, with its two large freshwater pools and extensive marshlands, the only permanent body of fresh water in an area of some 12,000 square miles of arid desert. This makes Azraq an important stopping, resting, watering and mating place for the thousands of species of migrating birds that journey every year between Africa, the Middle East and northern Europe. Part of the area has been fenced off and protected as the nucleus of the Azraq Wetlands Reserve.

A few kilometres north of the Wetlands, lies the sprawling, black basalt stone Azraq Castle where T.E. Lawrence (Lawrence of Arabia) headquartered with Prince Faisal while planning their final advance on Damascus during the First

Rooting system - Azraq

Fire room Qasr Amra

World War. Lawrence described the small city of Azraq as a "luminous, silky Eden" in his <u>Seven Pillars of Wisdom.</u>

The use of the hard, durable black basalt stone was common throughout northeast Jordan, where wood and other building materials were scarce. One of the doors of the castle is made of a single slab of thick basalt, which still swings on its stone hinges.

QASR AMRA

This is the most famous of the desert castles and the most impressive. Built as a bath complex and sporting lodge by the Umayyads, its fame lies in its still colourful - if scarred by time - frescoes covering the walls and vaulted ceilings. The animated scenes vary from larger-than-life wide-eyed dancing women to a series of panels depicting the animals of the desert that abounded in the eighth century.

Inscriptions scattered throughout the complex help unravel the mystery of Qasr Amra which seems to have been built by an Arab prince in the early part of the 8th century AD. Recent

Qasr Amra

excavations have revealed other nearby buildings, including a small, square, hilltop fortress and remains of residential buildings.

The original well and underground water system of the steam baths can still be seen.

QAST KHARANA

Southwest of Qasr Amra, about 60 kilometres southeast of Amman, is the best preserved and, in physical terms, perhaps the most imposing of the Umayyad buildings of the Jordanian desert.

Qasr Kharana, patterned after a Roman frontier fortress, is a large, square, two-storied building that was completed in 710 AD. The structure, with metres-thick walls, has two floors of living space with a third, open roofed area for unobstructed observation in every direction.

The castle is built around a courtyard which has been labelled both a stable and a courtyard for pleasure. Its beauty is in its simplicity, but the builder did allow for artistic expression in that there are some frescoes in the upstairs rooms, and the many arrow slots - opening in every possible direction so no enemy could approach in secret - are appropriately designed from the outside to look like the arrows they guide.

Qasr Kharana

Kharana caravan station

Kharana Place

QASR MUSHATTA

The biggest and most ambitious of the Umayyad desert castles is Qasr Mushatta. It was so big, in fact, measuring 144 metres on each side, that the Caliph Walid II never finished building it in the mid-8th century AD. Huge vaulted roofs, 23 semi-circular towers and the use of fired bricks as the only construction material gave the structure an imposing and majestic appearance.

It was originally covered with lavish carvings, but just prior to World War I, they were dismantled and shipped off by the Ottoman sultan Abdul Hamid to Kaiser Wilhem, who in turn had them sent to Berlin. Some of the best examples of the original plasterwork are on exhibition today at the Pergamon Museum in Berlin.

Mushatta Palace

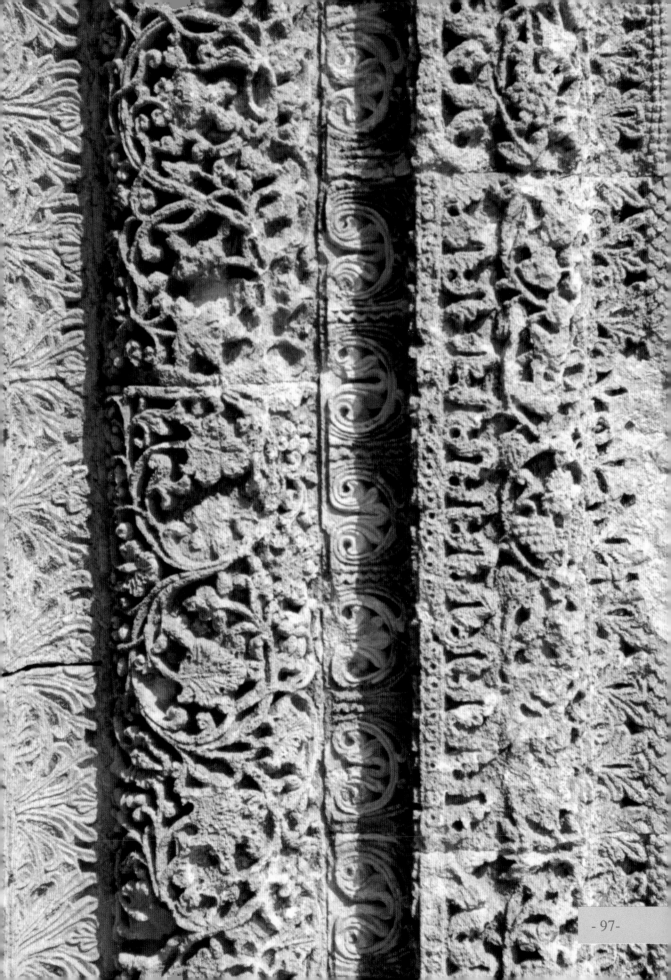

Index for Amman

JORDANIAN PAINTERS

ON JORDAN

Ali Jebri
Jerash

Princess Wijdan
Karak Castle

Ammar Khammash
Amman

Riham Ghasib
JEBEL AMMAN

Fuad Mimi
DEAD SEA

Suha Shoman
Petra